BILL KOEB

CARTOUCHE PRESS™
www.cartouchepress.com

Kings

1999

George Pratt

Introduction

I've known Bill for many years now. To tell you the truth, I don't even remember how we met, though I suppose it was at the San Diego convention years ago in the early nineteen-nineties. We shared a lot of similar interests, and had a mutual friend in Barron Storey, both of us at different times having been students of his, myself in New York, Bill in California.

Barron is a strong personality, his work no less so, and he influences people greatly once they have studied under him. At first the work is incredibly influenced by the style and thought of Barron, then, if the student is creative and possesses the inner resiliency to move on into their own thing, they do so. Bill has done this and it has been a pleasure to watch his vision and skill mature over the years.

I've seen in Bill a person who is deeply moved by events around him. He listens intently to the happenings in the world and then processes his concerns through his sketchbooks and his work. What is more, the imagery has become richer, the design more concise, his voice more powerful; he now says more with less.

In these pages you will find the many facets of Bill's personality and skill, from his initial, sometimes-cryptic sketches to more polished thoughts and full-blown paintings. It's enjoyable to watch the work progress, to see his thinking process from sketch to finish. What's more, you'll discover someone who is thrilled to be painting and drawing, for whom the very act is second nature.

Bill has now been blessed with a son, Gabriel, and I've been lucky enough to witness the turn in his sketchbooks and work to a more intimate, personal side of his nature. Being a father changes a man. Many artists, like Bill, dive headfirst into the experience, dirty diapers and all, because they learn something new about themselves. They see their priorities shift in a major, profound way and the work grows because of it.

Enjoy the journey.

George Pratt
Chapel Hill, NC

April 5, 2002

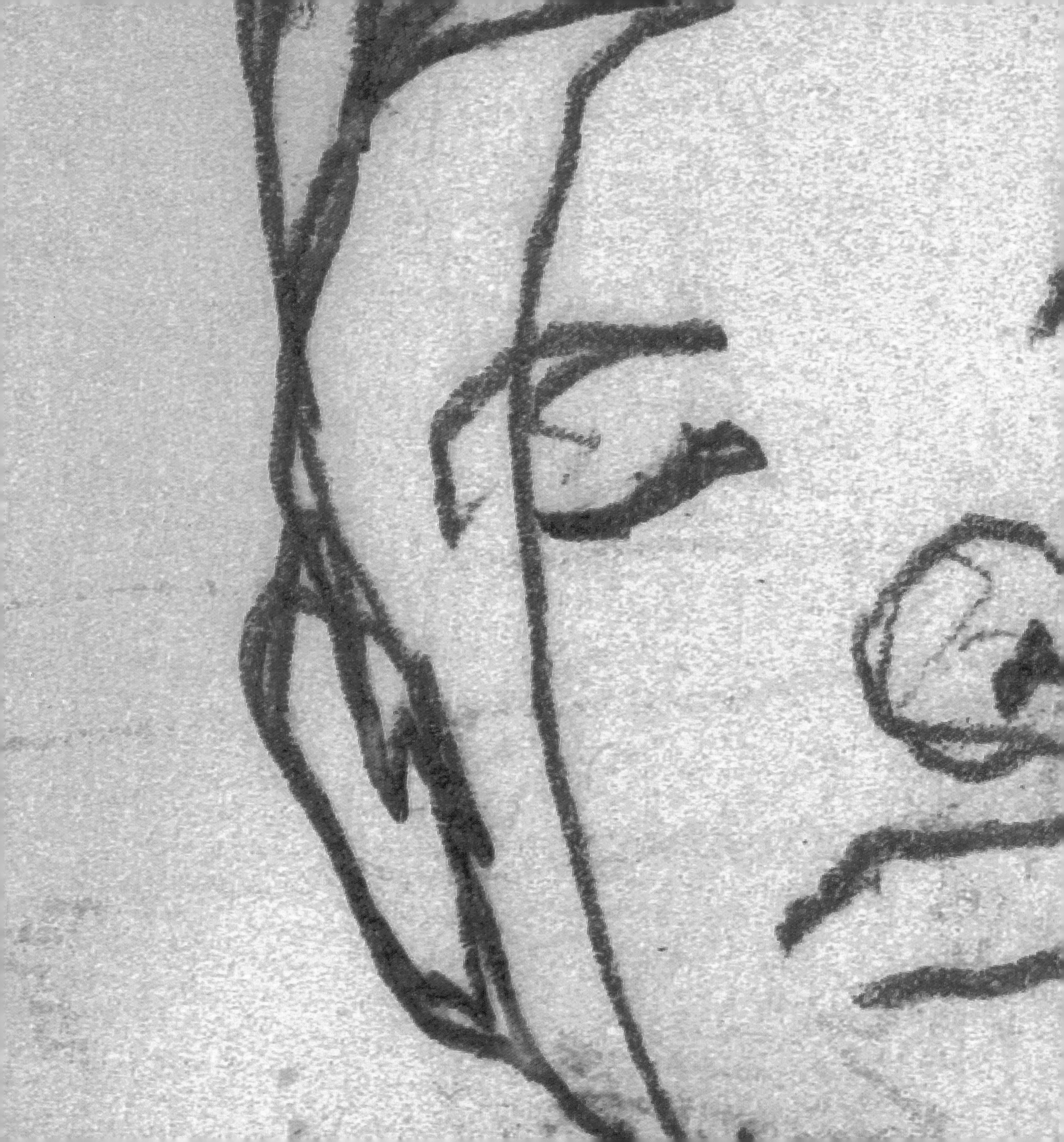

DRAWINGS

ReMEMORY I

all drawing is from memory. even when we look at something and draw it from life, it is our memory of the light that our eyes saw which we draw. light is the only thing we can see. the light hits the object, bounces back to our eyes, and is recorded in our brain. then we draw it . . .

memory

Falling Asleep

2002

this man was falling asleep on muni and waking up to the various bells and sounds the train made. he would start with his head up and his eyes closed, then a sound would awaken him, then, slowly his head would drop down again until the next sound stirred him from sleep. over the course of a few minutes i tried to capture this.

Two Heads

1998

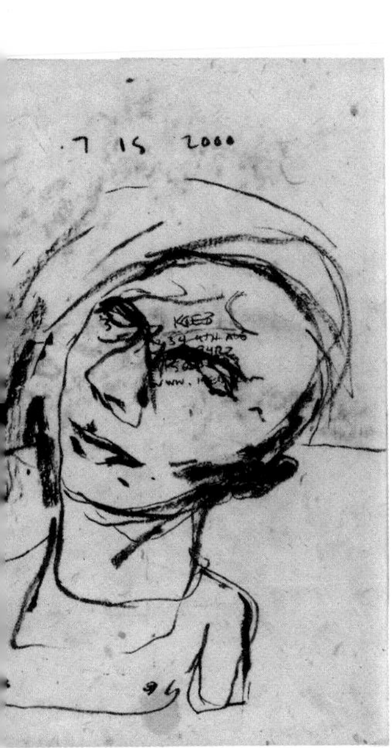

THE PEARL
THIS MUSIC MAKES ME FEEL SAD
9-21-2001

I LIKE THINGS IN THE CENTER

SWIMMER

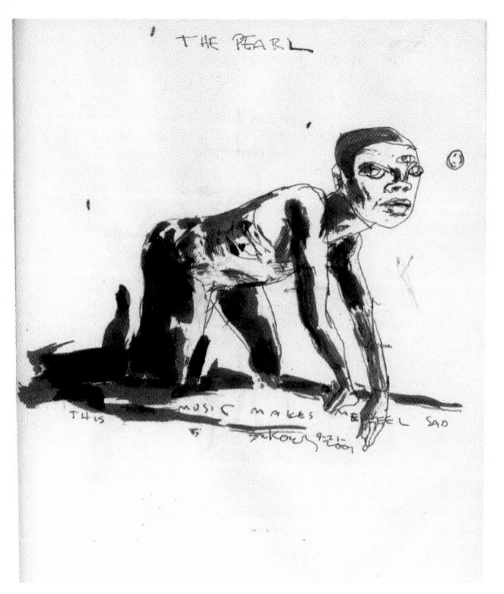

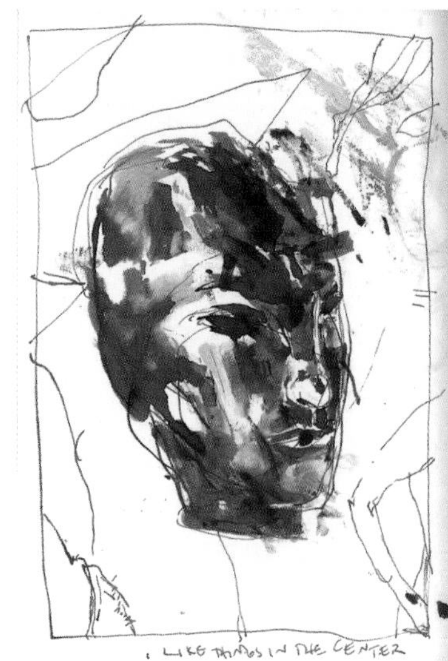

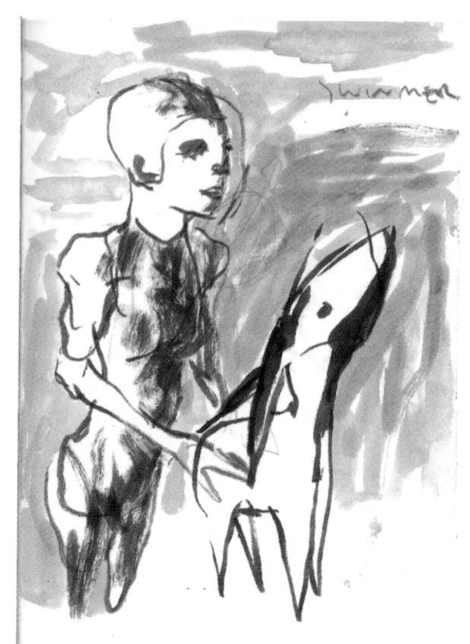

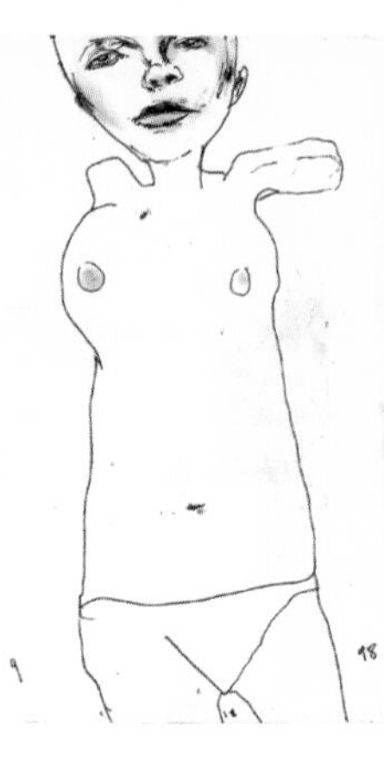

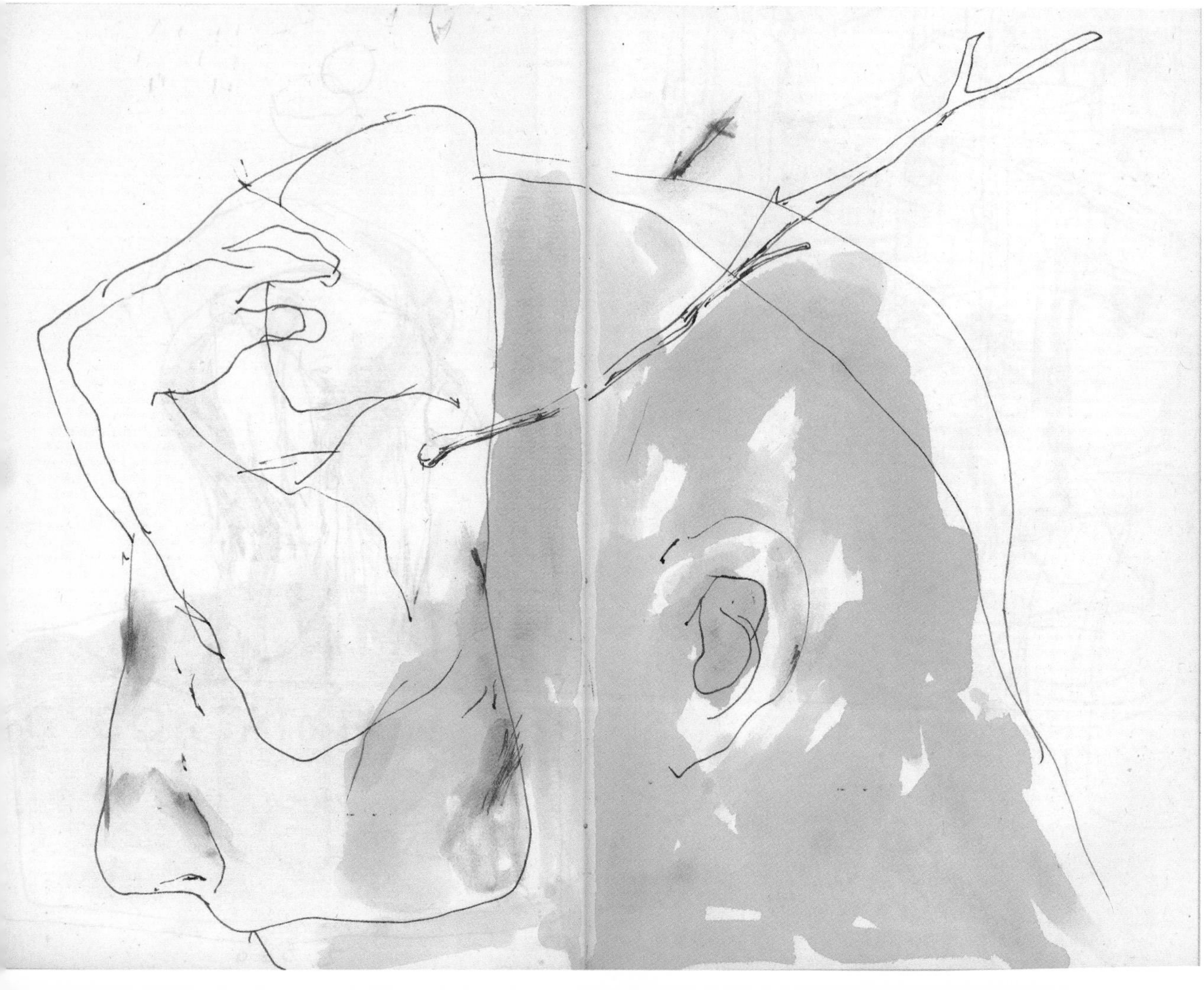

Deer

2000

Café Drawings

VARIOUS

Keith

2001

Summer Drawing

2001

GABRIEL

12-7-2001

Gabriel

2001

FATHERS

HARRY MANVILLE MOSES
GEORGE PRATT, BO

CHUCK TODD,

ANTONIO SANCHE

BILL NASSER,

FAULKNER, JOH

BOB OCHOA, BOB

RICK KOEB, RALP

MR. SCHULER,

CROWE, GREG T

RICK BERRY, G

WILLIAM ARTH

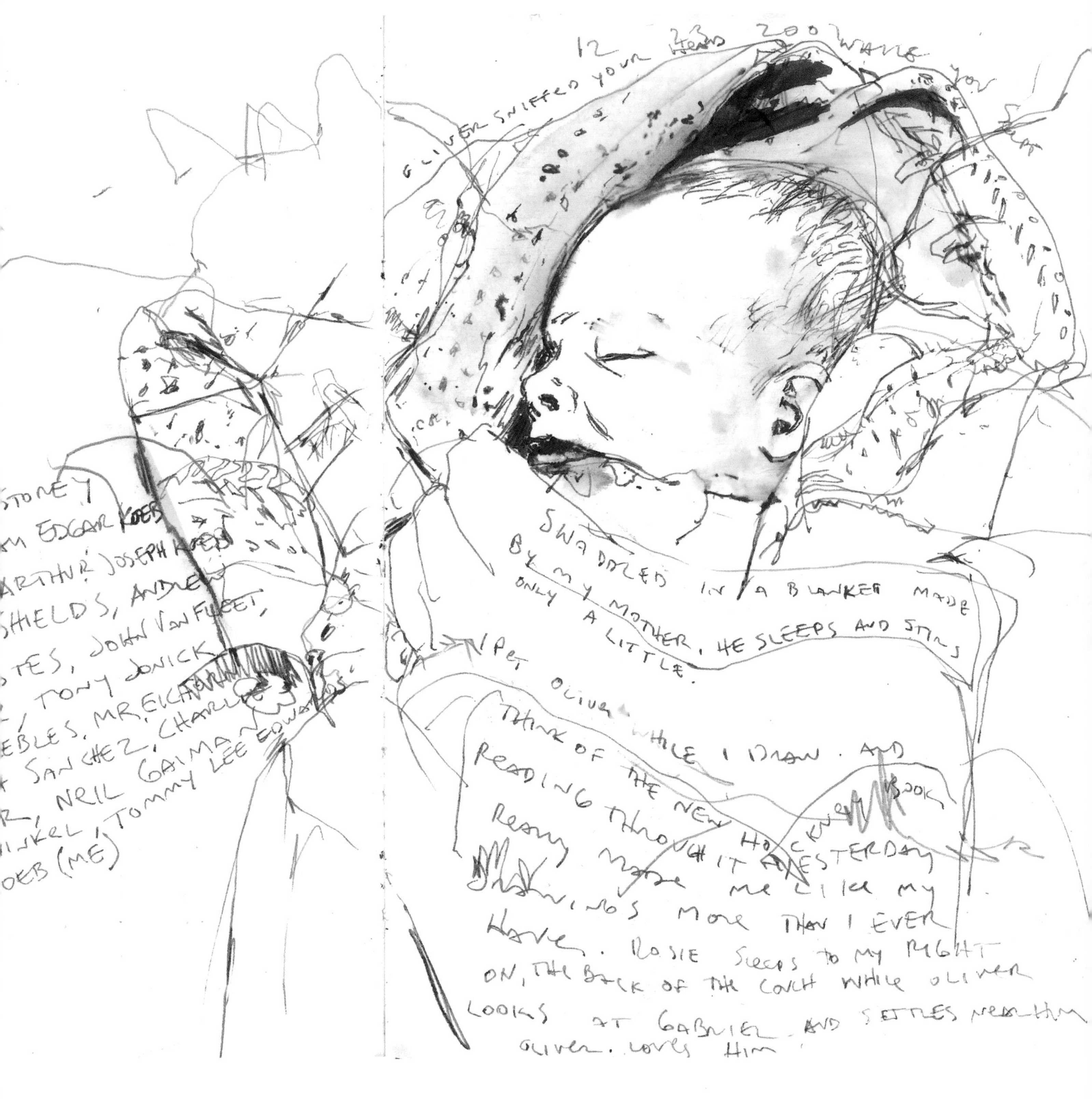

12 23 2007
OLIVER SNIFFED YOUR HEAD
STONEY
M EDGAR LOEB
ARTHUR JOSEPH LOEB
SHIELDS, ANDREW
TES, JOHN VAN FLEET,
TONY JONICK
EBLES, MR. ELCAR
SANCHEZ, CHARLIE
NEIL GAIMAN
INKEL, TOMMY LEE EDWARDS
OEB (ME)
SWADDLED IN A BLANKET MADE
BY MY MOTHER. HE SLEEPS AND STIRS
ONLY A LITTLE.
I PET OLIVER WHILE I DRAW. AND
THINK OF THE NEW HOCKNEY BOOK
READING THROUGH IT YESTERDAY
REALLY MADE ME LIKE MY
DRAWINGS MORE THAN I EVER
HAVE. ROSIE SLEEPS TO MY RIGHT
ON THE BACK OF THE COUCH WHILE OLIVER
LOOKS AT GABRIEL AND SETTLES NEAR HIM
OLIVER LOVES HIM

Julie and Gabriel
2001

F16

1996

7-13-96

KING TUT'S DESECRATED BODY.

F-16 CRASHED

A 4 year OLD
Boy DIED
THE PILOT
SURVIVED

9 / 11

2001

THE SECOND TOWER
THE SECOND PLANE 9 11 2001

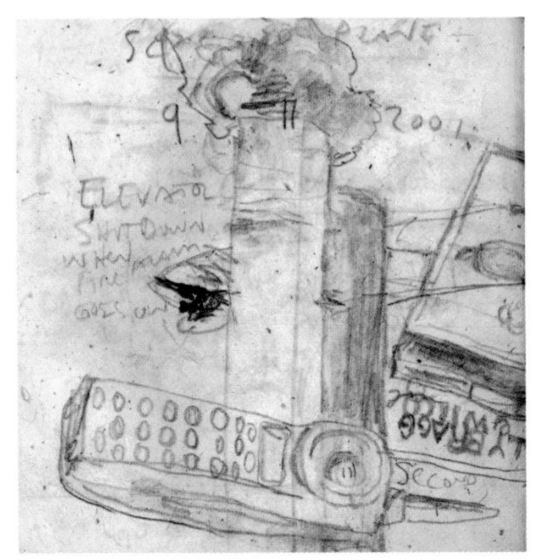
ELEVATOR
SHUT DOWN

as we left our flat on the beautiful and clear morning of september 11, my wife julie and i were told by our neighbor that someone had flown a plane into the world trade center towers. we listened with disbelief as he gave us this news. as we drove her to work and listened to the accounts of the attack on the radio, the horror of the attacks on the world trade center and pentagon became a chilling reality. i didn't know whether to continue on our way to her office or return home. after dropping julie off, i listened to various stations, trying to piece together the terrible sequence of events. as i looked around at other drivers, they all shared the same expression of shock and sadness at the radio reports of what was to be the most tragic terrorist attack in u.s. history.

when i arrived at home i sat in front of the television and watched the news for the next several hours with julie, who was sent home shortly after arriving at work. we sat there, not knowing how to respond, or what we were feeling. how does one respond when they witness an event so awful, so shocking, that it makes everything in their life seem small and trivial. the only thing that seemed to make any sense to do, was to sit and watch. i began to draw as a way of recording the events. with the distance of 3,000 miles and the distance that watching events on television brings, i know that mine is a pale record compared to the reality and impact of the attacks on those individuals who witnessed the terrorism firsthand, and who live with the daily reminder of the remains of the world trade center and the pentagon. but as a person who can draw, i feel that it is important to record what i can, and share it in the hope that in doing so, the world will become a little smaller.

in the pages of my journal i drew from the images on tv. what follows are some of the drawings that i made on that tragic and surreal day and on the days that followed.

bill koeb, 10.3.2001

THE PORCUPINE
BANG!

THE BABY RATTLE SNAKE
RUNS TO PARENTS TO DO DIRTY WORK

HOLD THE GOVERNMENT
TO THE SAME STANDARD
CITIZENS

FAZUL ABDULA MOHAMMED
FAZUL ABDULLAH
MOHAMMED

AMERICA'S
MOHAMMED
ATEF
MOST WANTED
IBRAHIM SALIH MOHAMMED YACOUB
IBRAHIM SALIH
MOHAMMED YACOUB

DONNA, 12 18 2000
FROM MEMORY OF SUNDAY NIGHT
HER BRUISING IS FADING, BUT HER BREATHING
IS SHORT AND SHALLOW,
SHE NEEDS MORE VISITORS
AUNT TONI CALLED,
SHE'S PRAYING FOR DONNA,

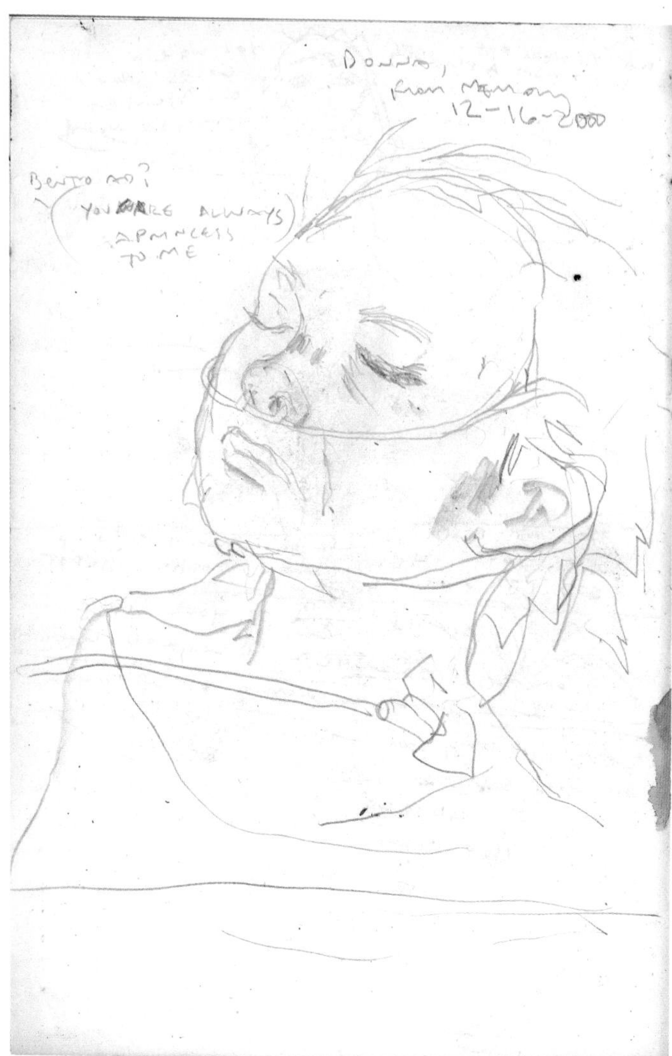
DONNA,
FROM MEMORY
12-16-2000
YOU ARE ALWAYS
A PRINCESS
TO ME

my sister donna was hospitalized from august 2000 until her death on october 22, 2002. since early childhood she suffered from diabetes which robbed her of part of her vision, her kidneys, and finally, her life. she had spent her final two birthdays in a hospital. it was the last of many stays in institutions over the past thirty years. these drawings were made of her while she was a patient at u.c.s.f. hospital, which was two blocks from my flat in san francisco. i was saddened by her illness, but grateful she was so close so i could see her on a daily basis. shortly before her death she very graciously consented to my use of these drawings, sight unseen, and to my writing about her here. it was our family's hope that someday she would be released from the hospital and go home. it is with love and sadness that i remember her.

Donna

2000

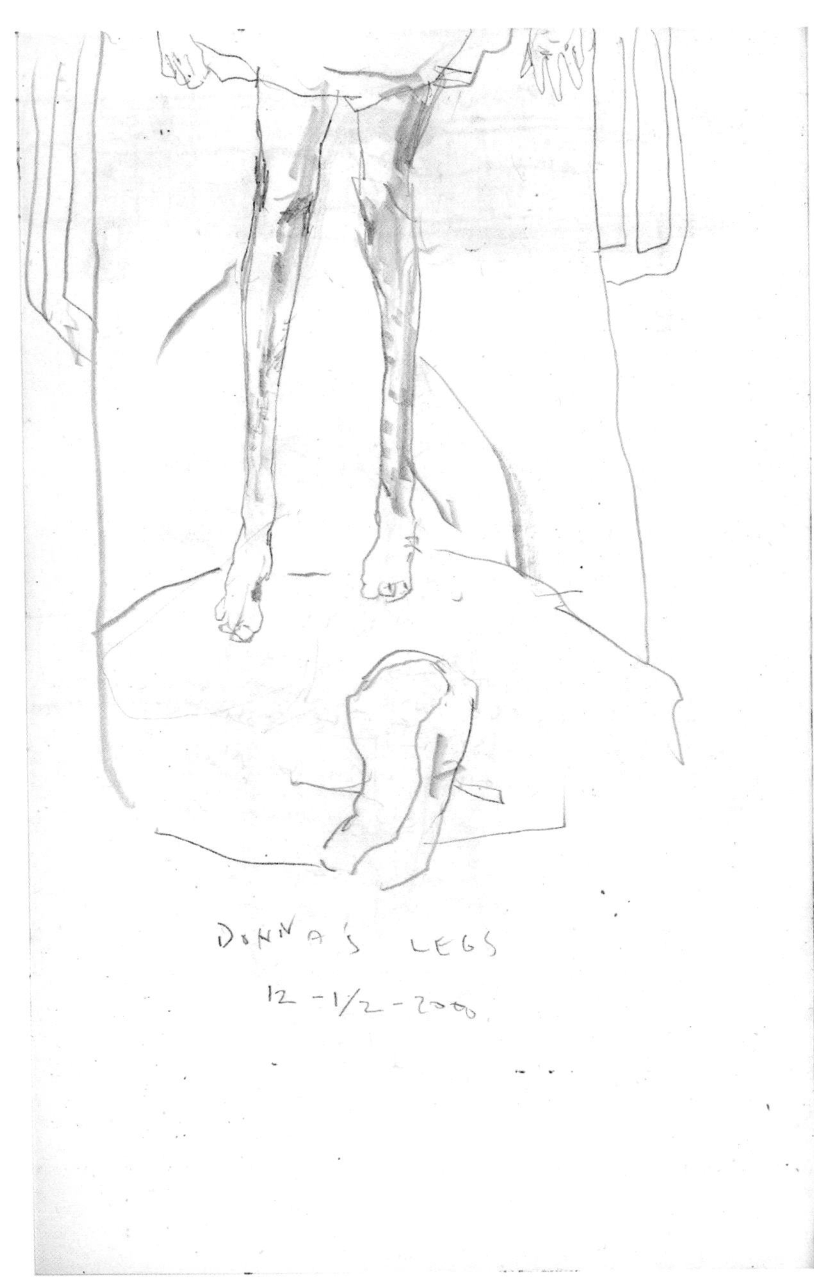

ILLUSTRA

IONS • PAINTINGS

ReMEMORY 2

jet lag

1996

Ophelia

2000

Knight

2000

Deerhunter

1998

Circus

2000

Summer

1999

Jennifer

2000

Besieged

2000

Bound

2000

Stick

1996

Batman & Robin

2000

Holocaust
2000

Betrayal

2000

Surrender
1999

Sundial

2000

Things to Remember

2002

War Zone

2000

Police Brutality

2000

Prayer
2000

Gabriel
2002

MONOTYPES

ReMEMORY 3

At Rest
1997

Aquarius
2001

Box
1997

Fallen
1997

Skull
1999

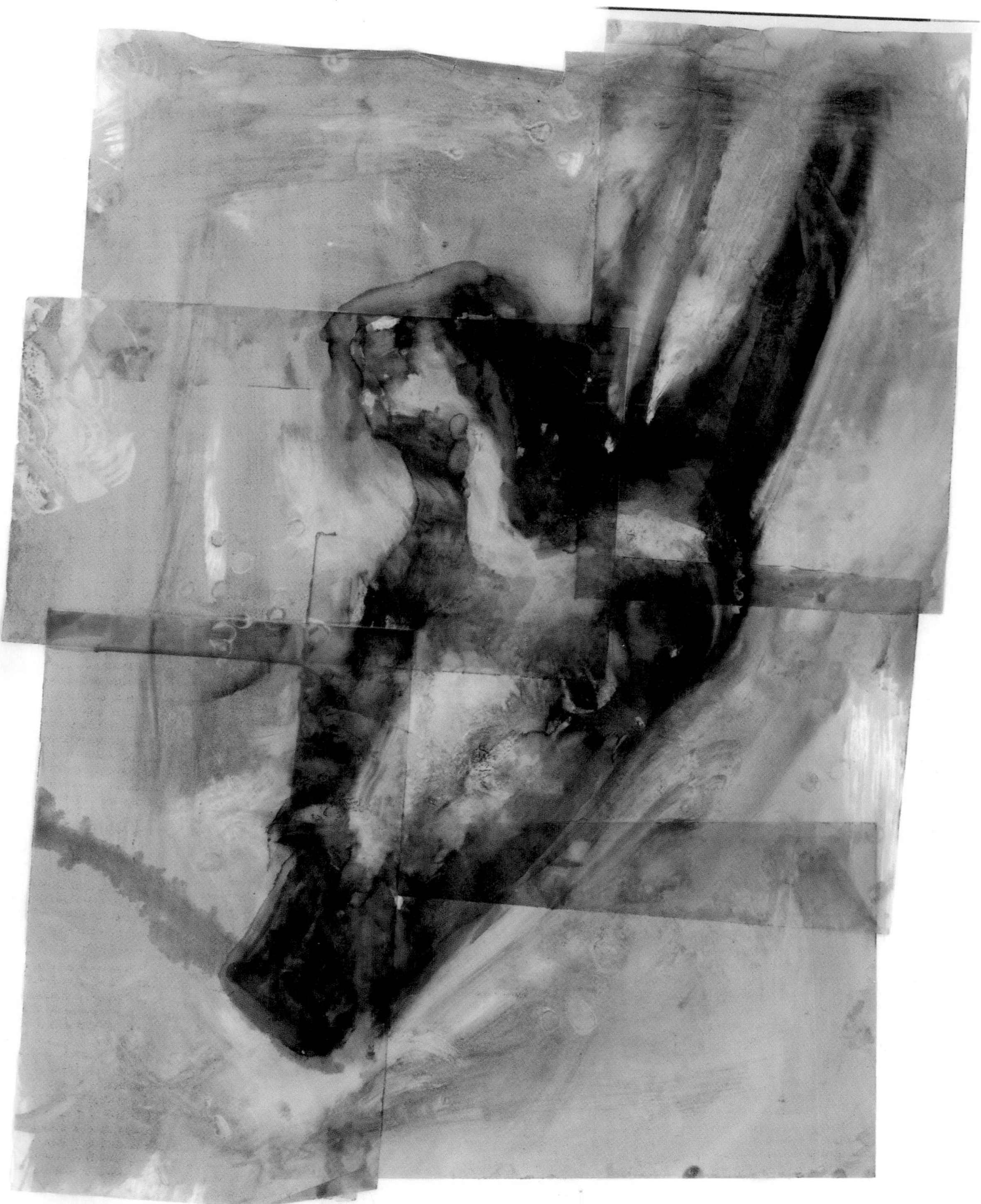

Oliver

1997

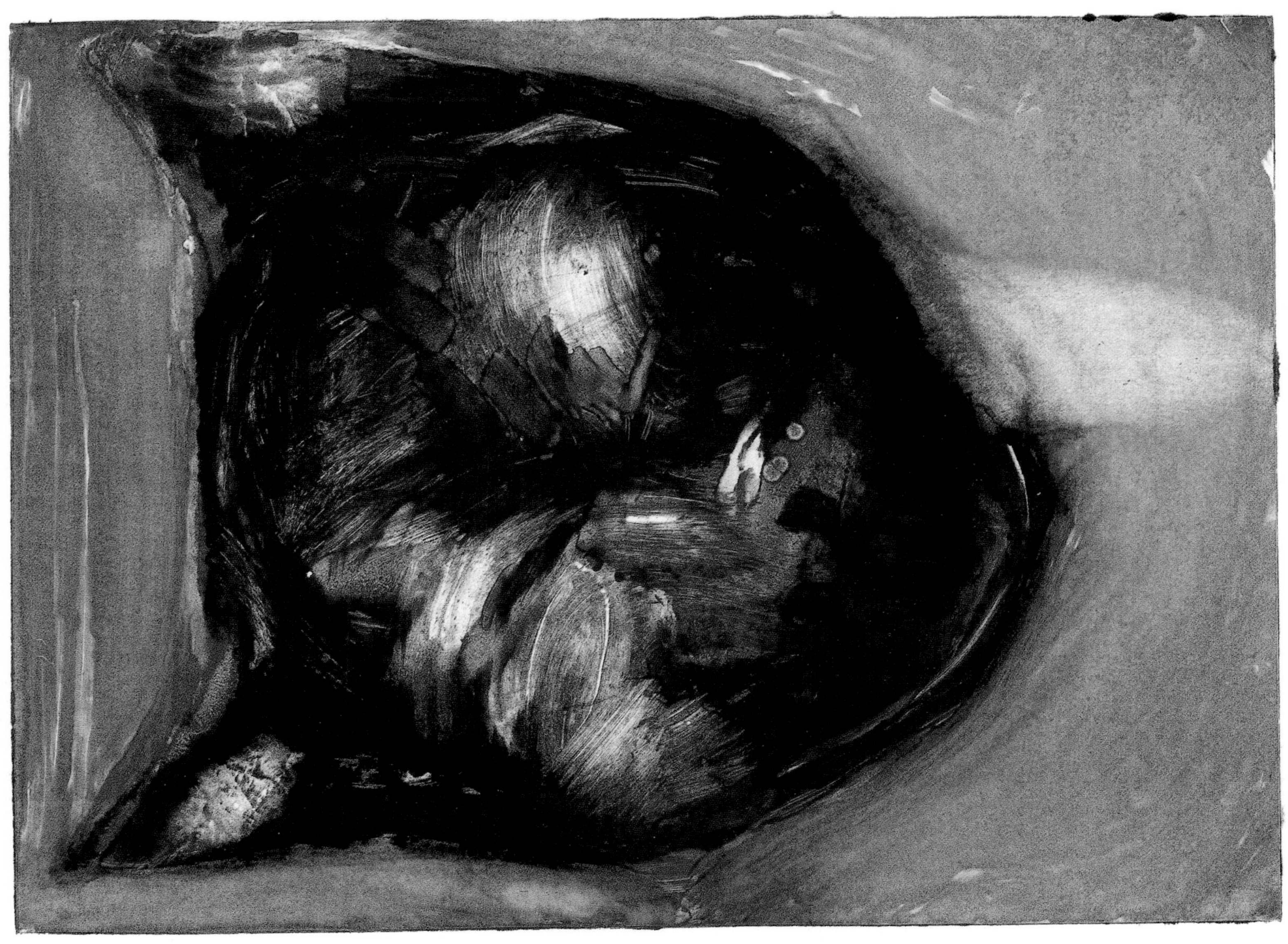

Julie
2002

Wrapped

2001

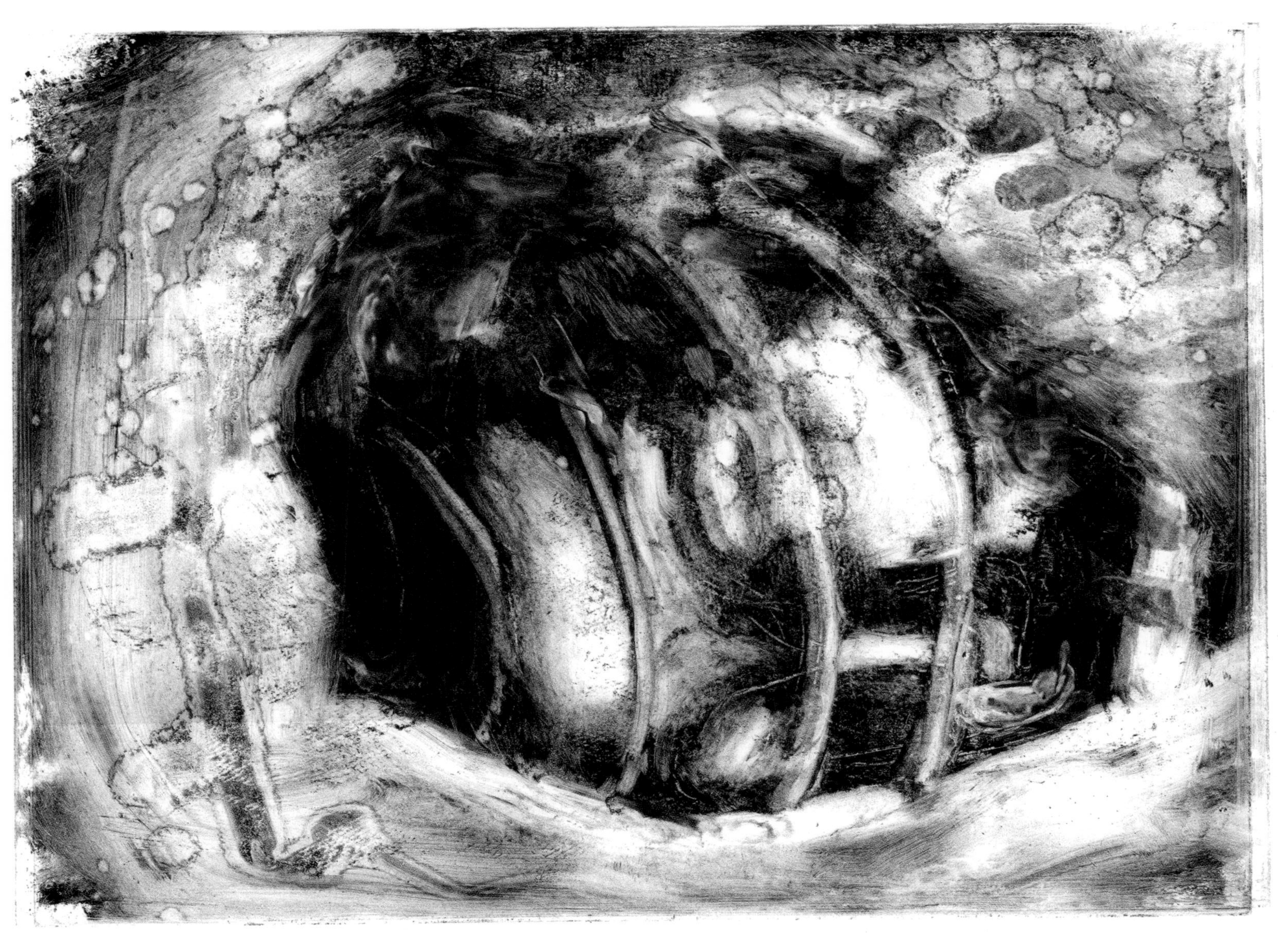

Nuclear Winter
2002

Summer Dress

1999

Kosova
1999

Kosovo II
1999

Doll
2000

Doll II

2000

Head I

1996

Emergence
2001

This book is dedicated to my wife Julie and our son Gabriel, without whom I would be half a man.

First of all I'd like to thank everyone who has shown an interest in my work. My parents who supported my desire to draw and paint, and all of you who I may never meet who support my work by buying this book. I'd like to thank everyone who helped make this book a reality: Anita, Gary, Sherri, George, Kevin, Meredith and Julie for looking at the work and helping me decide what to keep in and what to leave out. There were many more drawings that were left by the wayside, and without the invaluable help of Chuck Todd, I would still be sorting through piles of journals and drawings. Thanks to John for his words of wisdom. Much thanks also to Phil Reed for contacting me several months back with the offer to publish this book, and to Cartouche Press for giving me the chance to share some of my work. A special thank you to my late sister Donna for letting me include the drawings of her in this volume. And a special thank you to George Pratt for his input, help, and the kind words in his introduction for this rememory.

Photo by Julie Crowe 2002

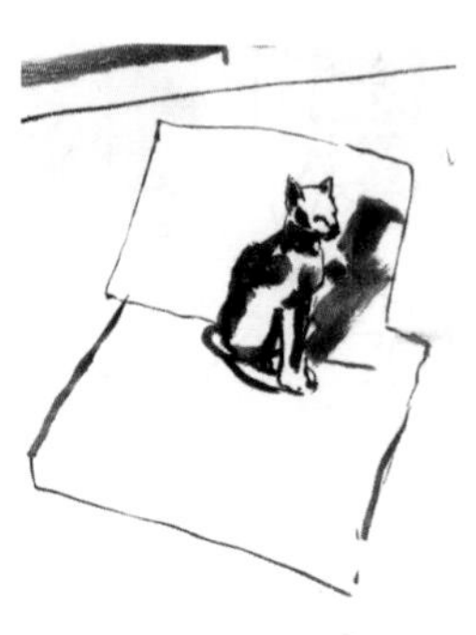

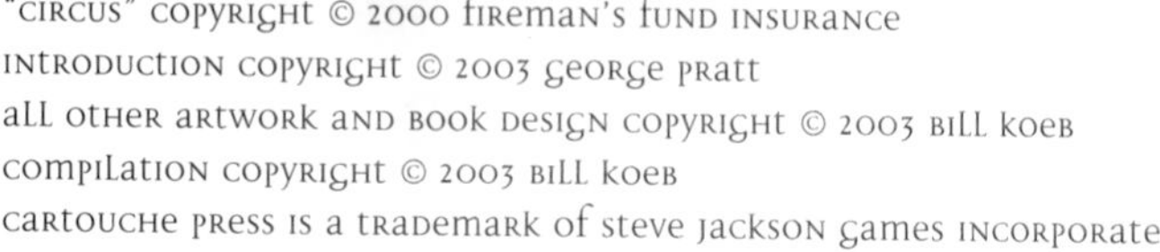

Editor in Chief ✠ Steve Jackson
Creative Director ✠ Philip Reed
Print Buyer ✠ Monica Stephens
Sales Manager ✠ Ross Jepson

CARTOUCHE PRESS™

ISBN 1-55634-631-X

1 2 3 4 5 6 7 8 9 10